ONE GOD

THE WAYS WE WORSHIP HIM

★ ★ ★ ★ ★ ★

ONE
GOD

THE WAYS WE WORSHIP HIM

by

Florence Mary Fitch

★

PHOTOGRAPHS CHOSEN
BY BEATRICE CREIGHTON

LOTHROP, LEE & SHEPARD CO.,   NEW YORK

Twenty-ninth printing, January, 1973

THIS BOOK

IS FOR

MY STUDENTS

AND

THEIR BOYS AND GIRLS

ACKNOWLEDGMENT

The author and editor appreciate the cooperation and interest of the many persons and organizations they have consulted while this book has been in progress. It would be impossible on one page to acknowledge individually everyone who has made a helpful suggestion, but the following people and groups have been consulted repeatedly and have been of the greatest assistance in the final editing of both pictures and text: The staff of the National Conference of Christians and Jews; Dr. Moses Jung of the American Jewish Committee; Dr. Ben M. Ediden of the Jewish Education Committee; Dr. Bernard Heller of the Sygnagogue Council; Rabbi Isidore Meyer of the Jewish Historical Society; Rabbi Solomon H. Metz of Adas Israel Synagogue; The National Council of Jewish Women; The Union of American Hebrew Congregations; Harold Schiff of the Anti-Defamation League of B'nai Brith; Father Joseph F. Cantillon, S.J., Chairman, New York Catholic Library Association; The Reverend J. Elliot Ross of the Paulist Fathers; The Reverend Charles M. Walsh, Acting Director of The Confraternity of Christian Doctrine, the Archdiocese of New York; The Reverend Justin Costello of Saint Catherine of Siena Church; The Reverend W. C. O'Laughlin, of the Sacred Heart Church, Oberlin; Maurice Lavanoux of the Liturgical Arts Society; The Reverend Albert J. Nevins of the Maryknoll Fathers; Reginald C. Caulfield of the Catholic School Journal; Ellen Johnson of the Oberlin Art Museum; The staff of Riverside Church; Dr. Philip C. Jones of the Madison Avenue Presbyterian Church; The Reverend George E. Nichols of the Church of the Heavenly Rest; The Reverend Oliver C. Weist of the West Center Congregational Church, Bronxville; The Reverend Alan Hackett; Eleanor F. Cole of the Pilgrim Press; Margaret M. Clemens of the American Baptist Publication Society; Mary Yocom, Assistant Professor of Education, Oberlin College; The National Council of Protestant Episcopal Churches; The International Council of Religious Education.

CONTENTS

PAGE

Why We Worship God 9

The Jewish Way 13

Jesus and His Followers 56

The Catholic Way 59

The Protestant Way 99

WHY WE WORSHIP GOD

Why do people go to church? Why do they read the Bible? Why do they pray?

The need of worship is no new thing. Ever since there have been men, they have felt themselves dependent on some power greater than themselves and have worshipped that power. In primitive times their place of worship was a high rock, a mighty tree, a little cave or a tent. Early primitive peoples thought there were many gods, who protected them and helped them fight their enemies. But now we know that there is only one God; there never has been any other, and all men are searching to find and to understand the one God.

For thousands of years men have prayed, to praise God for all His goodness, to find hope and comfort when they are sad, security when they are anxious, courage when they are weak. And for thousands of years God has answered, making them conscious of His presence as a Father more ready to give than they are to receive.

But even though they all worship one God, all people do not worship in just the same way. In America each person may make his own choice. Freedom of religion is one of the rights of free men. But most people follow the religion of their parents. There are many people who do not pay much attention to religion, but all are influenced by it, for they live in a country which was founded on faith in God.

It is not possible to present a universally true picture of religious observances, for customs vary in different communities and in different homes. This book describes the ways of worship which are usual among the majority of Jews, Catholics and Protestants — the traditional ways in which they worship the one God.

ONE GOD

THE WAYS WE WORSHIP HIM

"Have we not all one Father?
Hath not one God created us?"
Malachi 11:10

THE JEWISH WAY

The first people to understand that there is only one God and to set aside one day every week regularly for special worship of Him were the Jews.

Jews live in almost every country of the world — in America, in France, in Russia and even in China. The reasons for this are found in the long and very interesting history of the Jews. It begins with Abraham, the first person to be called a Hebrew. From a small tribe inhabiting Palestine, the Hebrews, who are thought to be descendants of Noah's son, Shem, and therefore Semites, grew and expanded. They migrated to Egypt and prospered until an ambitious king made them slaves. Then, under their great leader and teacher, Moses, who gave them their laws and government, they went back to Palestine. After many years of troubles, strife and battles, they were victorious in establishing themselves there. They became a great nation, which reached the height of its glory under King Solomon. But then the Hebrew nation was divided into two kingdoms — the kingdom of Israel, with its capital at Samaria, and the kingdom of Judah with its capital at Jerusalem. This is why the same people, originally called Hebrews, are sometimes called Israelites, and today are generally called Jews, from Judah.

After the division of the nation, there followed a long period of strife. Sometimes the Jews were victorious, as under Judah Maccabee; more often, because they were disunited, they were defeated. In the year 70, the Romans finally conquered the Jews and destroyed Jerusalem. The Jews no longer had a country and they dispersed throughout the world.

But a wonderful thing happened. Instead of forgetting their laws and customs, they loved them more than ever. In their

13

family life and their ways of worship they have followed the old established customs, generation after generation. Though in all other ways Jews conform to the life of the country which is their home, they have held on throughout the ages to their own religion, their own way of worshipping the one God.

THE SABBATH

According to the ancient tradition of the Jews, God created the heavens and the earth, the sea and all living things in six days and rested on the seventh. And God blessed the seventh day and made it holy. So they observe this holy day as a day of rest and of praise to God, the Creator of the world.

For them, more than for any other people, religion is bound up with the family life. This is seen in their observance of the Sabbath.

All Jewish holy days begin and end at sunset, because in olden times, before there were clocks, people told time by the sun. So the Sabbath begins with the coming of evening on Friday, and a good part of the day is spent preparing for it. Enough food is bought and cooked so that no cooking will be necessary on the Sabbath. The house is given a special cleaning and the mother or servant is busy preparing the soup, fish and chicken. Sometimes they bake the bread, the Hallah, at home, cutting the dough into strips and braiding it into the special shape of the Sabbath loaves.

The delicious smells of the cooking and baking in the kitchen make the children more eager for the coming of the Sabbath, the day that crowns the week. They have their work too. They help clean the house and set the table for the Sabbath meal. They put the best linen cloth on the table, arrange the flowers, and polish the silver. They place the two heavy brass or silver candlesticks, the engraved silver Kiddush cup filled with wine, and the two twisted loaves of Hallah, covered with a snowy white embroidered cloth. At last everything is ready and the mother lights the candles.

This is the age-old ceremony that ushers in the Sabbath. In some families she covers her head. She stands silently before the table for a few moments, then she spreads her hands above the flames and holds them before her face as she prays, first in Hebrew, the ancient language of her people, then in English:

"Blessed art Thou, O Lord our God, King of the universe
Who hast sanctified us by Thy commandments
And commanded us to kindle the Sabbath lights."

Then almost silently she adds, "May our home be consecrated, O God, by Thy Light."

The family watches for the father's return from the service at the synagogue and wonders whom he will bring with him. In olden times whenever a Jew found himself in a strange town on Sabbath Eve, he could be certain that some one in the synagogue would invite him home to share his family meal, and the Jewish people have always been famous for their hospitality.

The children rush to meet their father, greeting him with "Good Sabbath." As soon as the men have washed their hands, saying a little blessing as they do so, the family gathers in the living room and sings a greeting to the Sabbath:

"Welcome, Sabbath Angels,
Angels of Peace."

Then the father reads from the Proverbs the praise of women, as a special honor to his own wife. The children stand before him and he lays his hand upon each and blesses them one by one. After this the family goes to the dining room.

At the table the father lifts the cup of wine and pronounces the Kiddush, the Sabbath Prayer. He pours off a "cup of blessing," a small portion of wine, for each member of the family. Everyone washes his hands and then a blessing is said; they sit down and the meal is served.

The family may be poor; the food may be scanty; the week's work may have been hard; but as a rabbi said long ago, "The spice of the Sabbath makes the plainest food taste better than any feast." Often songs are sung between courses and the meal becomes very gay.

Sometimes the conversation turns to how the old customs began. The children like to ask their father questions, even though they already know the answers; or the father may question them to see how well they remember. They tell of the Ten Commandments which their ancestors promised that they and their children would keep; one of these was, "Remember the Sabbath day to keep it holy — in it thou shalt not do any work." The servants and the beasts of burden, the ox, the ass, were all to rest too, and any stranger who might be on a long journey was to find safe shelter and peace among them. One day in seven to rest! when in most of the world the poor slaves and beasts toiled from daylight to dark, year in and year out! No wonder that an old legend records that God said to Moses, "There is a magnificent gift in my treasure chamber, the Sabbath is its name, and I shall give it to Israel."

At the close of the meal the family sings a psalm and says grace. Then they go into the living room where they may settle down to read, or talk. Everyone relaxes in the way he prefers.

Many Jews interpret strictly the commandment: "Thou shalt not do any work." They will not drive a nail, or carry a burden, not even a book, or walk beyond the city limits longer than what is prescribed as "a Sabbath day's journey," or do any one of the many other things definitely forbidden. One of the most important restrictions was not to make a fire, because in early days this involved much labor. Today many Jews will not strike a match or even turn on the electric light. The father does not smoke on the Sabbath.

Saturday morning the family attends the service in the synagogue. In the afternoon the father and older sons may go again for a short meeting, in which there is reading and discussion of some great Jewish writing. "The Sayings of the Fathers" is most often used; it is a collection of wisdom from the teachers of many centuries.

One of the best liked stories is that of Hillel, a famous scholar and head of an academy in Palestine. Everybody knew of his gentleness and patience. One day a Roman came to tease him, and asked him to teach him the whole of the Jewish religion while he stood on one foot. Hillel never was angry even when people asked foolish questions: he tried to turn their foolishness to good account. So he replied: "Do not do unto others what thou wouldst not do unto thyself. This is the whole law; all else is explanation."

By these little ceremonies the Sabbath is made different from the rest of the week. Everyone has a chance to rest, and in resting "to acquire an additional soul."

Late in the afternoon, as it begins to grow dark, the children watch for the first three stars, and when they have seen them they announce, "The Sabbath is over." This is the signal for the family to gather around the table for the Havdalah, the ceremony which marks the end of the day. Then the lights are flashed on and everyone calls out, "A good week to you."

This custom, which the Jews established so long ago, of setting aside one day in seven for rest and worship, has become a general practice throughout the Western world. Christians observe Sunday, Moslems Friday, but the spirit of the day is the same. Even those who do not think much about religion look forward to a different day, a day for the best dinner of the week, a day for the family to get together, a day to welcome friends and strangers, a day of refreshment before beginning another week of work and play.

RELIGION IN THE HOME

Another way in which family life is bound up with religion is in the care with which the mother observes the dietary laws in the preparation of food.

In olden times, as in some countries today, conditions were unsanitary; the weather was often hot and damp and there were

Reading the Psalms in the synagogue

no refrigerators. As a result there was much sickness. The ancient Jews discovered certain rules of health and thought them important enough to make them religious ceremonies. Their teachings say that it is necessary to be cleanly in habit, to eat wholesome food, and to lead a good life, and so keep a healthy soul in a healthy body. That which Jews may eat, according to these rules, is "kosher"; what is unfit for food is "trefah."

There are many of these rules specifying just what is kosher and what is not, and these laws are very significant to Jews. They have been observed for many centuries, and they have become a vital part of the religion.

Many Jews observe them today not only because they are sound sanitary laws but still more because they are religious laws, part of the long established Jewish way of doing God's will.

It is forbidden to mix meat and milk products, so there is no butter on the table with a meat dinner, and no creamed chicken. In homes where the dietary laws are most carefully observed, there are two sets of pots and pans, dishes and silverware, for preparing and serving meat meals and milk or cheese meals. The mother chooses dishes that are quite different, so that they will not be mixed carelessly, and keeps them on separate shelves.

The father presides over the family worship and both he and the mother tell the children about the history and teachings of their ancestors. They are proud that they are Jews as they listen to stories of the heroes of their people—Moses, Samuel, Ruth, David, Elijah, of Bible times—and in later times the sweet-tempered Hillel, the great rabbi and physician Maimonides, and intrepid explorers and discoverers, generous philanthropists, noted scientists and artists, from earliest times to the present.

The first religious ceremony for the little Jewish boy occurs when he is eight days old. On this day he is circumcised and given his name. The family and friends gather in the home for the circumcision, the Brit Milah, a very old ceremony which brings him into the covenant which has bound God and Israel ever since the time of Abraham. A godfather holds the child and an official called the Mohel performs the operation. The father offers his thanksgiving: "Blessed art Thou, O Lord our God, King of the universe, Who hast sanctified us with Thy commandments and enjoined upon us the circumcision." Then he announces the name of his child. The friends respond with good wishes, a prayer is offered over the wine, and there are refreshments for all the guests.

There is a ceremony for girls, too. As soon as possible after the little girl is born, preferably on the Sabbath, the father goes to the synagogue and is called to the altar, where a special prayer of blessing is read in her honor. "He who blessed Sarah, Rebekah, Leah and Rachel, Miriam the prophetess and Esther the queen, may He bless this dear girl. Let her be called (the full name is given) in a lucky hour. May she grow up in health and peace, and may her parents live to celebrate her wedding."

Jewish babies are seldom named for any one living: usually they are named after friends or relatives who have recently died. Biblical first names are the favorites with Jewish parents. The most honored family names among the Jews are Cohen and Levi, for Cohen indicates a descendant from Aaron, the first priest in Israel, and the Levites were those who assisted at the altar.

The first lullaby a Jewish baby hears when his mother puts him to bed, may be this old, old one:

> "O! hush thee my darling, sleep soundly, my son,
> Sleep soundly and sweetly till day has begun;
> For under the bed of good children at night
> There lies, till the morning, a kid snowy white."

> "We'll send it to market to buy Sechora (goods)
> While my little lad goes to study the Torah.
> Sleep soundly by night and learn Torah by day,
> Then thou'lt be a Rabbi when I have grown gray."

Then when her baby is older, a big boy of five or six, she may tell him about the Torah, which means "teaching." The Torah is the first five books of the Bible, known as the Books of Moses. It contains stories, poems, laws, speeches and other records of the early history from Abraham to Moses. It is written in Hebrew and it is the most sacred part of the Jewish Scriptures.

The most important part of the Torah is the "Shema," and one of the first sentences a child is taught to read in Hebrew is the beginning of the Shema: "Hear O Israel: the Lord our God, the Lord is One."

When the Shema was written, almost everyone believed that there were many gods, gods of storm and thunder, gods of rain and of the sun, gods of sickness and of death. Idols were made to represent these gods and sacrifices were offered to them so that they would do good and not harm. The religion taught by Moses was the first to say that idols do not mean anything, that there are not many gods, but only One. Some few persons perhaps had thought so before, but they never tried to make all the people believe it and stop being afraid of unfriendly gods and spirits. Moses taught not only that there is no God but One, but that He is a God to be trusted. For the Shema continues: "Thou shalt love the Lord thy God with all thy heart and with all thy soul and with all thy might." This is one of the two most significant teachings of the Torah. The other one is: "Thou shalt love thy neighbor as thyself."

When he is six years old and starts school, the Jewish child also goes to the Hebrew school. Here he learns to read and understand the Hebrew of the Scriptures and to recite prayers. He also learns about the symbols and ceremonies associated with each festival. Before Passover, the festival which comes about the same time as the Catholic and Protestant festival of Easter, he may help set up a miniature table containing the symbols of the Seder service. Perhaps his class dramatizes the story of Moses leading the children of Israel across the Red Sea. As he grows older he is introduced to the history of his people and learns the laws that govern their life.

22

The Torah used in the Synagogue is always copied by hand on parchment and rolled, just as scrolls were before the days of printed books. The rollers are of wood. The upper ends of the rollers are ornamented and have silver caps with bells attached. In the picture the caps have been removed and can be seen with the breastplate that belongs on the velvet wrapper in which the Torah is kept when not in use. A pointer ending in a small hand with the pointer finger extended is also fastened to the scroll and is used by the reader as he follows the words across the lines. Hebrew is written from right to left across the column, just the opposite from English. When one column is finished, the reader turns the rollers to the next column which is to the left.

He learns to read

and to write Hebrew

25

and to recite prayers.

BAR MITZVAH

The most important day in a boy's life is the Sabbath following his thirteenth birthday, for then he becomes Bar Mitzvah, a Son of the commandment. He becomes responsible for his own behavior. From now on he will fast and pray as his father does, and go with him to the synagogue.

His father and rabbi have given him careful preparation and he has practiced putting on the tephillin. These are two little square leather boxes attached to long narrow straps of black leather. The boy places one of the tephillin on his left arm, holding it in place with the strap, repeating words which his father and his father's father have said each morning as they made themselves ready for prayer: "I bind this as a sign on my hand, as a memorial of Thy outstretched arm." The other box is placed in the middle of the forehead and also secured with a strap. The boxes are often very beautiful in workmanship. Inside each box is a narrow parchment upon which is written the Shema, and other verses from the Bible. The passage ends: "These words thou shalt bind for a sign upon thy hand and they shall be as frontlets between thine eyes."

The boy receives many presents for his Bar Mitzvah, among which are beautiful new tephillin, and a man-sized talith, the prayer shawl with tasseled fringes at the four corners.

Jewish boys for two thousand years and more have been taught to cover their heads in the house of worship and whenever they pray, as a sign of respect to God. In Christian churches it would be thought strange for a man not to take off his hat, but the Catholics teach that no woman may come into a church with her head uncovered. A Catholic priest covers his head on many occasions, but never when celebrating Mass. In the British House of Commons, a man always puts on his hat when he addresses Parliament. The sense of what is fitting varies according to custom.

Beautiful new tephillin, and a man-sized talith . . .

"I bind this as a sign on my hand, as a memorial of Thy outstretched arm."

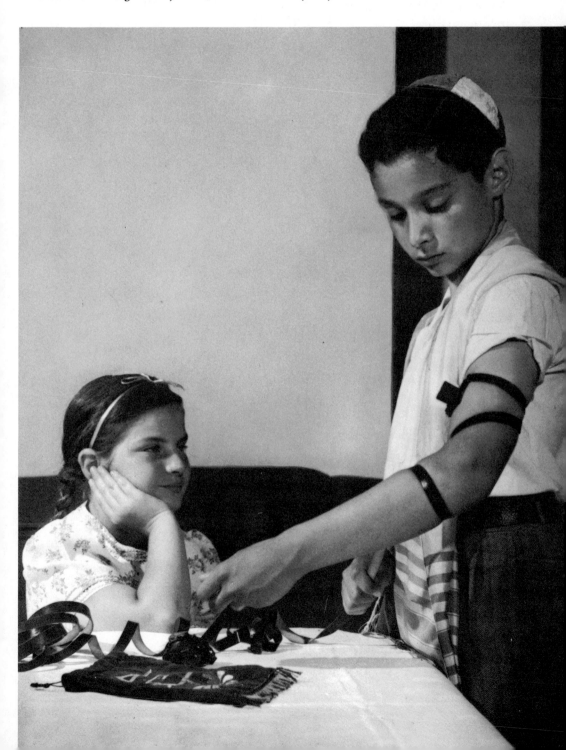

THE SYNAGOGUE

On the day the boy is to become Bar Mitzvah the family goes proudly to the synagogue. Never has the boy been so interested in everything about the building. Now, in a new sense, he is to belong to it; he is formally entering the congregation of Israel.

Synagogue means a place of assembly and the synagogue is used for any gathering the people may wish to have. But first of all, it is the House of God. It is so built that the worshippers face east, that is, toward Jerusalem. The large room has pews and a platform at the front, in the middle of which is the reading desk.

On the back wall of the platform is the Sacred Ark, a cabinet in which the scrolls of the Torah are kept. Above the Ark, two lions, symbols of the tribe of Judah and the house of David, hold stone tablets upon which are engraved the Ten Commandments. A heavy velvet curtain embroidered with the Shield of David, a six-pointed star, covers the Ark. Before it hangs the Eternal Light, a lamp never allowed to go out.

At the entrance to some synagogues the family divides. The mother and sisters go to the gallery reserved for women. On this occasion they are glad to be where they can see so well. The boy, dressed in new clothes, takes a seat with his father. He unfolds his talith and covers his body and head with it, praying quietly. He then places it over his shoulders. His uncles and cousins and other friends come to the service and each one covers himself in the same way.

The choir of men and boys sings an opening hymn, made up long ago of verses taken from various books of the Bible; then the cantor chants the call to prayer: "Praise you the Lord, to whom all praise is due." There are many chants and prayers and responsive readings from the prayer book. These are in Hebrew, but the prayer book gives a translation into English in a parallel column so that everyone can follow the service. Each familiar phrase takes on new meaning for the boy.

Then comes the moment for which all this has been preparation —the reading of the Torah. The little bells tinkle as the scroll is carried to the reading desk and taken out of its velvet case. Seven portions of the Sidrah, the part of the Torah assigned for this particular Sabbath, are read by the cantor and seven men are called up to the Torah in turn, to say a blessing before and after the reading of each portion.

Then the Bar Mitzvah boy is called to the reader's desk; sometimes he himself reads the concluding verses of the Sidrah and chants another selection from the Prophets. In some synagogues the boy is invited to give a brief speech which he has himself prepared. He thanks his parents and teachers for their care and training and pledges loyalty to all their instruction.

The rabbi usually gives a little talk to the Bar Mitzvah boy and his parents. Then the cantor proceeds with the chanting of the service. Afterwards the boy receives congratulations and the relatives go to the home for further celebration.

The word rabbi means "my teacher." The rabbi is the friend and counselor of his congregation. He is not set apart from others as are priests in many religions. His clothes are like those of other men, although in the pulpit he may wear special vestments. It is right for him to marry and have children, that he may be an example of normal living. In most synagogues he is paid by the congregation in order that he may be free to give all his time to teaching.

In other religions the sacred books were the concern only of priests and scholars; this was true also in the early history of Israel. But more than two thousand years ago, Jewish leaders began to spread education among all the people; they wanted every Jew to be intelligent and to think. They taught them to read and study the Scriptures. The first sermons ever preached were those in Jewish synagogues. Anyone learned in the law might be asked to interpret the Scriptures. Hebrew was the language commonly spoken then and it is still used in the synagogues. No matter where a Jew lives or what language he speaks, the use of Hebrew

Guard of honor for the Torah. Usually it is composed of very important men in the synagogue, but sometimes it is boys who are Bar Mitzvah or older. Only an exceptionally good student is allowed to read the portion from the Torah.

Rabbi addressing an inter-faith gathering

reminds him that he belongs to the congregation of Israel; and if he ever travels far and comes to a synagogue in a strange land, he will hear familiar words and songs and feel at home.

1777483

CONSERVATIVE AND REFORM JEWS

Some Jews have modified many of the observances of the laws and customs of their people and so they are called Conservative Jews. Their religious practices vary between the strict observances of traditional Jews and the simpler character of Reform worship. Generally, however, they follow more of the Orthodox customs.

Reform Jews have adapted their ways to those which are more general in western countries. They call their places of worship temples and families sit together. Men take off their hats as the Catholics and Protestants do.

There are organs in Reform temples and choirs are nearly always composed of both men and women. In the liturgy Hebrew is used but most of the prayers are in English as is the sermon. They have confirmation for both boys and girls.

Confirmation does not necessarily occur on the thirteenth birthday. It takes place when the boy or girl completes the course of study which the rabbi considers essential. Confirmation is held on Shavuoth, the day that commemorates the giving of the Law, the Ten Commandments, to Moses on Mount Sinai over three thousand years ago. The confirmation ceremonies usually follow the festival prayers of Shavuoth. This is a fitting occasion for such a ceremony because for the class, as for the Israelites at Mount Sinai, it publicly affirms their allegiance to God and their avowed intention of living by His laws.

Yet in spite of these differences all Jews are bound together by their belief in the one God and their pride in their long history.

Learning the Hebrew alphabet

Learning Jewish history

Confirmation class in a Reform temple, showing Ark in background. The Hebrew verse over the Ark means "Know Before Whom Thou Art Standing." The two words which appear above the scrolls of the Law in the Ark mean "The Crown of the Law" and refer to the primacy of the Torah, or Law, in the Jewish faith. The six-pointed

star which appears on the pulpit is the "Shield of David." Hanging over the altar is the Perpetual Light, which represents the eternal light of faith; on either side are the seven-branched Menorahs, symbolic of those in the Temple at Jerusalem. The rabbi is at the left, and the cantor of the congregation is at the right.

Temple Emanuel

HIGH HOLY DAYS

The Jewish New Year begins in the fall with Rosh Hashanah, the First of the Year. One of the most impressive parts of the synagogue service is the blowing of the shofar, a trumpet made from a ram's horn. In olden times it was blown from the housetops to announce the arrival of every Sabbath, to summon the people for any important assembly, to call to arms in time of war. Now it is seldom heard except at New Year and Yom Kippur.

Rosh Hashanah is the day of judgment. According to the old tradition it is the day when God inscribes in the Book of Life His judgment upon the actions of each person, and when everyone should pass judgment on his own life. Rosh Hashanah is kept for two days. Apples dipped in honey are served in the home to express the hope that the New Year will be sweet and happy. The children love to have two holidays when they can stay home from school but that is not the reason for the longer celebration. When the Jews all lived in the little land of Palestine, everyone could see the signal fires that were lighted to announce that the new moon had been seen; but as they scattered to other countries, because of the difference in time, it was not possible to be sure just when the month had begun, so they kept two days. Orthodox and Conservative Jews still follow this custom.

The days between Rosh Hashanah and Yom Kippur (the Day of Atonement) are called the Ten Days of Penitence. These are very holy days, for the rabbis taught that these were ten days of grace during which time, by penitence, prayer and charity, an unfavorable judgment in the Book of Life might be changed for the better. The final day of this judgment period is Yom Kippur, the tenth day of the new year. At the end of this day the Book of Life is definitely sealed. Yom Kippur is a solemn day of fasting from sunset to sunset. The ambition of Jewish boys is to be brave and strong enough to fast the entire twenty-four hours. At the age of six or eight they may fast for only one meal. The older they grow the longer they fast, and by the time they are thirteen they must fast all day.

Even those who do not attend the synagogue regularly go to the service on this holy day. They confess all wrongdoing of the year and ask forgiveness for themselves and for all their people. The older ones remain in the synagogue all day. The children come and go. The final service takes place toward sundown. There is a short but very impressive ceremony and one long loud blast of the shofar is blown to mark the sealing of the Book of Life, the end of the fast and the holy period, and the real beginning of the new year. The congregation leaves, hoping God has heard their prayers of repentance and that they have been inscribed for life and happiness in the year to come.

FESTIVALS

From New Year on, throughout the year, come many other festivals. There is Succoth, the Feast of Booths, "a time of rejoicing." In smaller towns each family has a little arbor in the yard which the children help build. Here they eat their meals for a week. In the city where so few families have gardens, branches and fruit may be put over an apartment balcony. Usually a city synagogue has a large succah and holds parties in it for the children. This commemorates the time when their ancestors were protected by God in the wilderness on their way from Egypt to Palestine and had no permanent homes. It also reminds them of life in Palestine where farmers make little booths in the midst of their fields and vineyards in which they live in the fall to protect the ripening fruits against thieves.

The booths are also a symbol of the insecure lives of many of the Jewish people, who still search for a safe home. But most of all this festival recalls God's goodness and faithfulness so that "Seed time and harvest never fail."

Sounding the ram's horn

Gathering corn for a succah

Children marching around the synagogue and singing songs in praise of Simhat Torah

HANUKAH

The holiday children like best is Hanukah, the Festival of Lights. It comes, as does the Christian festival of Christmas, in December when the short days of winter begin to lengthen, when once more the sun gives men assurance that spring is not far behind. For eight days the beautiful Menorah, holding its eight candles, stands in the window. At sunset the father lights the candles; in some families, one the first night, two the second, and so on; in other homes all are lighted every night. The youngest child may be the little priest for the first night, lighting the candle and reciting the blessing.

It was at this season of the year that the Jews won the first great fight for religious freedom. The Syrians, who had ruled Palestine, tried to force the people to give up their religion and adopt that of their conquerors. For three years the temple in Jerusalem was in the hands of the enemy. Then the valiant little Jewish army, led by Judah Maccabee, drove them out. The temple was cleaned, a new altar built, a large Menorah candlestick was lighted, and other ceremonies carried on. Once more the Jews were free to worship their own God in their own way.

No wonder that the children love this week. They put on masquerades and plays to illustrate the story; they play games dramatizing the exploits of Judah and his courageous band. There are plenty of parties, with pancakes, the special Hanukah food. Best of all, it is the time of gifts, when everyone remembers his family and friends.

Another festival that is a favorite of children is Purim, which comes at the beginning of spring. It commemorates the ancient victory of the Jews over the hated tyrant, Haman. The celebration is a gay and happy one marked by the telling of the story of Esther and Mordecai, the delicious specially baked Haman tarts, and the masks, costumes and noisemakers that are all a part of the festival.

The Menorah is lighted for Hanukah.

Hebrew anagrams is one of the games played during Hanukah. These boys have spelled out "We are lighting the candles."

A Menorah in an Israeli park

PASSOVER

The Passover comes in the early spring. In the synagogue service on Passover morning the Song of Songs is read; "The rain is over and gone; the flowers appear on the earth; the time of the singing of birds is come and the voice of the turtle is heard in the land."

In the home great preparations are made. New clothes are bought for everyone and the house is cleaned from attic to cellar. The dishes that are never used except for Passover week are taken from the top shelf and washed; the Passover silver is rubbed until it shines. There must not be a bit of dust anywhere; everything must be clean and pure.

Many families keep up the old custom of hunting for leaven on the evening before the Passover begins. During Passover week, only unleavened bread is used, so the father searches the house to make sure there are no bits of ordinary bread anywhere. For the sake of the old ceremony the mother has hidden little pieces for the father to find. The children always enjoy the hunt.

The most wonderful meal of the year is the dinner on Passover Eve. It is called the Seder, which really means order of service, because every part of the evening follows the old, old customs. The table is even more festive than it is for the Sabbath dinner, and unleavened bread in square flat cakes called Matzoth takes the place of the Hallah. There is a large platter holding the Seder symbols: a roasted lamb bone to represent the sacrificial lamb; a roasted egg, symbol of life and hope; horseradish roots and parsley for the bitter herbs to symbolize the bitterness of losing one's rights, and a mixture of apples, nuts, and wine to suggest by its red color the bricks which the slave people in Egypt were forced to make.

The father's chair is heaped with cushions, a reminder of the old custom of reclining at meals enjoyed by those who were free, but not by slaves; and everyone feels gay and carefree at the Seder.

"the flowers appear on the earth . . ."

At sundown the family in festive mood gathers about the candle-lighted table and the curtains are drawn to shut out the world. Never are the children so conscious of their Jewish heritage as on this night. For thousands of years their people have kept this feast; at the same time in almost every land countless Jews are observing it. They may be poor, they may be in exile, they may be persecuted, their meal may be most frugal, but all of them know that they are a part of a great company who are remembering the past and praying that all Jews may again be free.

The father lifts his glass and blesses the wine; then all drink. A basin, a pitcher of water, and a towel are passed for the ceremonial washing of hands. After this everyone dips a bit of parsley in salt water and eats it. Then proudly the youngest child, if he is six years old, asks "the four questions," for which he has been carefully drilled.

The children listen as if they are hearing it for the first time as the father reads the story from the Haggadah, although it has been told in every Jewish household ever since there has been a Jewish people. In the Torah it is written: "When thy son asketh thee in time to come 'What mean the ordinances which the Lord our God hath commanded?' then thou shalt say to thy son, 'We were Pharaoh's bondmen in Egypt, and the Lord brought us out of Egypt with a mighty hand.'" So the father tells them how Moses asked Pharaoh to let the people go free, but Pharaoh only made them work harder.

Then Moses told them to make ready quickly for a long journey, to bake their bread without waiting for it to rise, to kill a lamb, put its blood on their doorposts. During that night the firstborn son in every Egyptian home died, but the angel of death passed over the homes that had been marked with the blood of the lambs. This is why the festival is called the Passover. Frightened and sad, Pharaoh ordered Moses to take his people away. Therefore, the Passover is the festival of freedom. During the long recital four cups of wine have been served to celebrate the four stages of the redemption of Israel.

Symbols of the Seder Service

The Four Questions.

"*Wherein is this night different from all other nights? For on all other nights we may eat either leavened bread or unleavened, but on this night only unleavened.*

"*On all other nights we may eat other kinds of herbs, but on this night only bitter herbs.*

"*On all other nights we need not dip an herb even once, but on this night we do so twice.*

"*On all other nights we eat sitting upright, but on this night we recline.*"

When the story is finished, the food is brought in. The first course is hard-boiled eggs served with salt water, for tears and hope have always been the lot of Jews. Then come fish and fowl and all the other good things and for dessert each one has a little piece of a matzoth.

Seven weeks after the Passover comes the Festival of the First Fruits, or the Feast of Weeks. Later it was called Pentecost, from the Greek word for fifty, as it began the fiftieth day after Passover. These seven weeks had been the time in Palestine for gathering the harvests of barley, lentils and wheat and this, like Succoth, is a thanksgiving festival. Many families decorate their homes gaily with flowers and green foliage. But the historical association is the more important, for it is believed to be the day when the Ten Commandments were given to Israel, the beginning of the law not only for them but for the many nations which have learned from them. This holiday is observed chiefly in the synagogue and the school.

All these traditions, holy days, festivals, customs and laws make up the way of worshipping God that is known as the Jewish religion.

JESUS AND HIS FOLLOWERS

Almost two thousand years ago, Jesus was born in Bethlehem in Palestine, a Jew of the royal line of David. Some believe that He is God Himself, in human form. His life was so important that we date our time from His birth. B.C. means before Christ and A.D. stands for the Latin words Anno Domini, in the year of our Lord.

Jesus was one of the greatest teachers of the world. He taught in the synagogues, by the sea shore, and on the mountain side— wherever He found people who wanted to listen. As a devout Jew, He respected the Torah, but He did not observe all of its minute requirements.

Like rabbis of his day, before and since, He wanted people to do what would please God; but He believed, as many Jewish prophets did, that God does not care as much about the observance of the many laws of the Jewish tradition as He does about the love and loyalty of His children.

God is King of kings, Ruler of the universe, but He is also the Father of every individual; He asks that each man treat every other as a brother, loving, serving, and forgiving him as there is need. Jesus believed that God's will will triumph on earth, but He needs the help of men. When He was asked: "What commandment is the first of all?" He answered: "Thou shalt love the Lord thy God with all thy heart and with all thy soul and with all thy strength. And the second is this: Thou shalt love thy neighbor as thyself. There is no other commandment greater than these." He showed this love by His deeds; yet some people disagreed with His teachings and opposed Him.

Jesus celebrated the Jewish feasts with His friends. The last meal He ate with them was the Passover. After they had finished, He took some of the bread, broke it, and passed it to them, and said: "Take, eat; this is my body." Then He gave them a cup of wine, saying: "This is my blood, drink of it." They wondered then what He meant; many people still are not quite sure; but they understood that He was about to die and that He wanted his Spirit to live on in them.

The next day, which was Friday, He was crucified by His enemies and buried by His friends. The old tradition accepted by most Christians is that early Sunday morning two of His disciples and several women came to the tomb and found it empty; and an angel said: "He is not here; He is risen"; and later He appeared to His friends.

The disciples, who a few minutes before were sad and hopeless, were filled with joy. Their Master was alive! They began to spread the news. People met in little groups, in the temple and in their homes, to talk about Him and the way He had taught them to live. They were sure that His Spirit was with them and would work through them. They called Him the Christ, which is derived from the Greek word for anointed, because they believed that He was the one anointed to bring in the Kingdom of God. Soon his followers were known as Christians.

On the first day of each week they met to celebrate their joy in His resurrection. Sunday became the special day of worship for Christians, although as Jews, they still observed the Sabbath.

Among those who joined the Christian group in Jerusalem there were many who had come to the capital city to celebrate Pentecost and then went back to distant homes. Through them the story of Jesus was widely spread to other lands. About twenty years later a young Jew named Paul, went from Jerusalem through Asia Minor, Greece, and on to Rome, preaching about Jesus. Other people besides Jews were interested and accepted the new faith. Christianity no longer belonged to the Jews alone. From this beginning it has grown until it has become a world religion. Today there are Christians among every race of people.

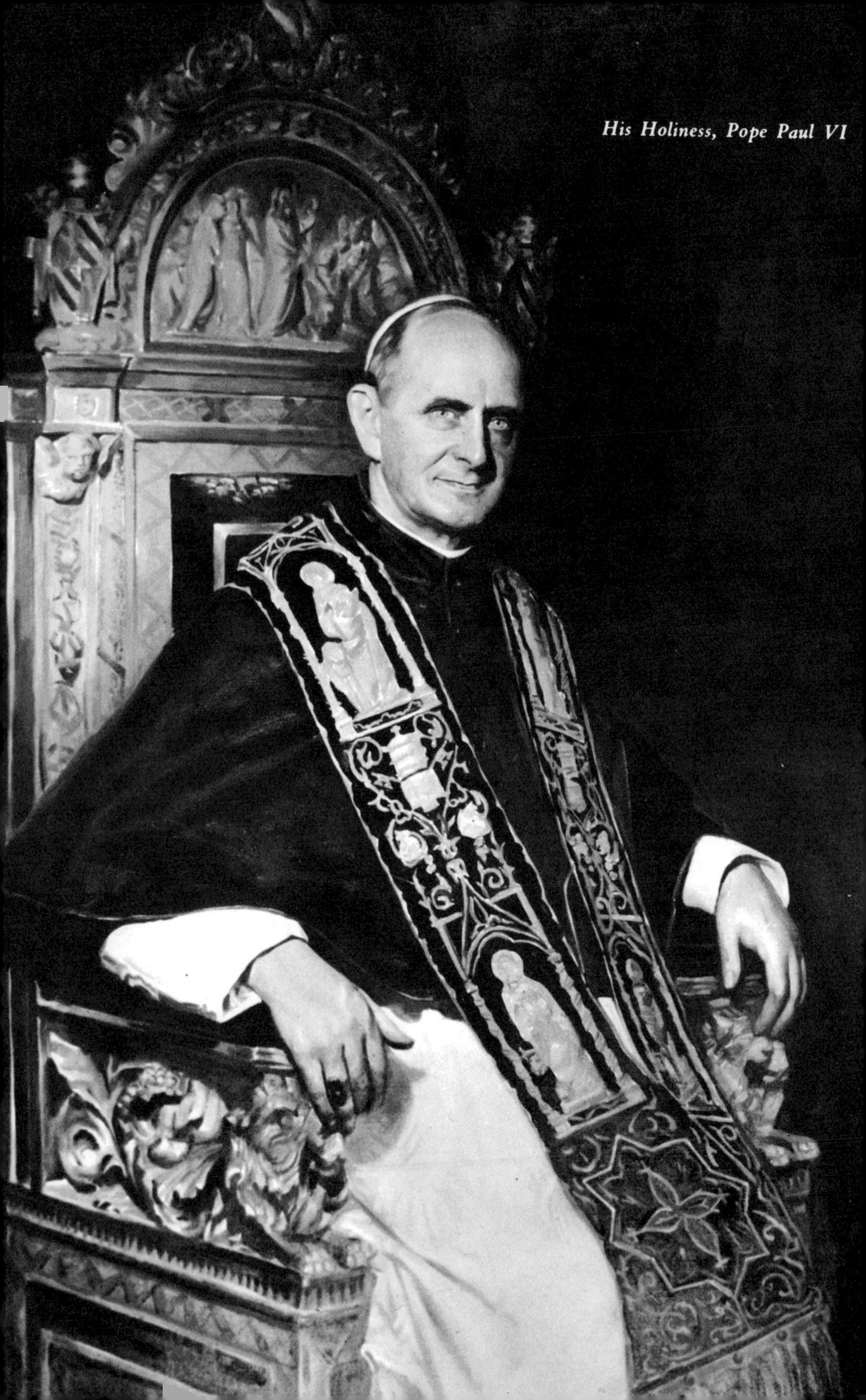

His Holiness, Pope Paul VI

THE CATHOLIC WAY

Jesus had wanted His work to go on after He left the earth, so He told His twelve closest friends to go into all the world to carry the good news which He had brought. They became more than disciples, which means learners; they were apostles, those sent out as missionaries. According to Catholic teaching, Peter established in Rome the central church to hold together the many scattered groups of Christians. This was called the Holy Catholic Church, for Catholic means universal.

All Catholics believe that Jesus is God Himself, and that He gave Peter authority over the Church. Peter was the first Bishop of Rome. When he died, he passed on his authority to his successor as have all the bishops since. Like Peter, each Bishop of Rome is the head of the Church, and is called the Pope, the Holy Father.

There are many bishops, and each has responsibility for a particular country or state. Through the "laying on of hands," they receive divine power as a special gift from God and they pass this power down to every priest and to every member confirmed in the Catholic Church.

The Catholic believes that the Church gives all that he needs for his religious life. From her he learns what he is to believe and how he should live to please God; he comes to know the traditions and the correct forms of worship; his heart is satisfied through her sacraments; his will is trained by her discipline.

"The laying on of hands" ceremony, first step in becoming a priest. The bishop's gloves are removed for the anointing of the priest's hands with oil.

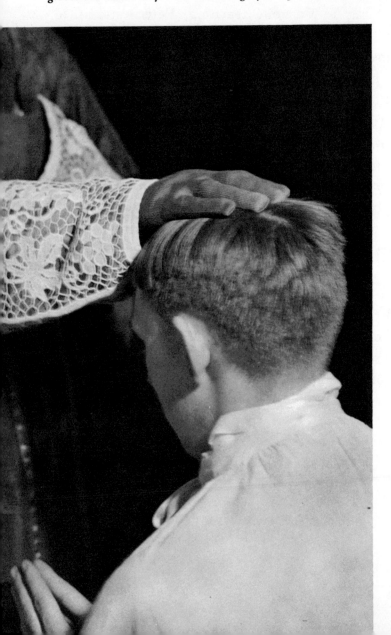

Prostration at ordination ceremony

St. Peter's in Rome.

BAPTISM

The Catholic Church teaches that baptism is necessary for the salvation of the soul, so parents plan for the baptism of a newborn baby within the first month of its life. This frequently comes on Sunday afternoon, followed by a gathering in the home of relatives and friends who bring small gifts and congratulate the parents. The sacrament of baptism is called christening. In Catholic families it is customary to name the child after some saint, perhaps the one on whose feast day the child was born or is baptized.

The baby is taken to the church by godparents, chosen by the parents. They are there to promise to help the child grow into a strong Christian man or woman, if the parents fail to help, or if they should die.

The baptismal font is near the entrance of the church to show that baptism is the first step in the Christian life. Water is the symbol of purity, and baptism, by removing sin, makes the child worthy of belonging to God.

The godparents hold the child over the font, and the priest takes a small pitcher filled with the specially blessed baptismal water and pours it upon the baby's head three times, calling the child by name and saying "I baptize thee in the name of the Father and of the Son and of the Holy Ghost." Then he anoints the top of the child's head with holy oil in the form of a cross, to show that he is a Christian, safe in the Church of our Lord.

The words of the baptismal ritual suggest the ways God helps those who are entrusted to Him: He gives them a Father's protecting care; He lets them know His love through the life of His Son, Jesus; His spirit is the Holy Ghost, "closer than breathing, nearer than hands and feet," which keeps them conscious of His presence and eager to do His will.

HOME TRAINING

As soon as the child is old enough to notice what is around him, he sees in his home a picture or image of Christ upon the cross, which is called a crucifix, and another of the gracious woman, whom he is taught to call Mary, the Blessed Mother of God. He comes to love them as members of his own family. When his mother holds him up before the statues, she makes the sign of the cross over his head, heart, and shoulders saying the words that were said at his baptism: "In the name of the Father and of the Son and of the Holy Ghost."

When he can talk he likes to try to say them with her, and he learns for himself prayers which he has heard his parents say:

"Our Father, who art in heaven, hallowed be Thy name.
Thy Kingdom come. Thy Will be done on earth as it is in
heaven.
Give us this day our daily bread
And forgive us our trespasses as we forgive those who
trespass against us
And lead us not into temptation, but deliver us from evil.
Amen."

and

"Hail Mary, Full of grace.
The Lord is with Thee.
Blessed art thou among women; and blessed is the fruit
of thy womb, Jesus;
Holy Mary, Mother of God, pray for us sinners
Now and at the hour of our death. Amen."

When he is a little older, he has a rosary like his mother's, a string of beads, alternating one large and ten smaller ones, with a crucifix at the end. By this he can count his prayers, saying "Our Father," for each big bead and a "Hail Mary," for each smaller one. There are five such groups. He says them all three times to complete the rosary, but not all in one day.

THE CHURCH

When he reaches his sixth birthday the child begins to go with his mother to Church. The church may be a splendid cathedral rising above all the homes of the city, or a little wooden building set up in newly settled country. It may be very beautiful and have rich decorations, or be plain and almost bare. There is great variety in Church architecture. Many Catholic churches are rectangular in shape like the traditional Jewish synagogue, but the typical form is that of the cross, for the cross is the central symbol of Christianity.

When a child enters a church built in this style, he finds a broad aisle down the center, and the first thing he sees is the altar at the farther end. On either side there are pews for the congregation. This part of the building is called the nave, which means ship and suggests that there is safety and peace in the Church always, as a ship is safe even when there are storms at sea.

The nave ends where it meets the cross-section, the transept, which may have aisles and pews in the arms. Often a dome or spire rises above the place of crossing, lifting the heart of the worshipper toward heaven.

The child may be told that the center aisle which leads to the high altar is to remind him of the path of life which leads to God.

Usually there is a smaller altar on either side, or, in a larger church, two or more side chapels. One of these is dedicated to the Blessed Mother Mary and contains her statue; the other to any saint, but most often, the Blessed Joseph, who is still the protector of the faithful, as he was of Mary and her Holy Child.

There are pictures on the walls of nave and transept and in the stained glass windows. There may be statues on pedestals or in niches, inside the church and outside. Many centuries ago few people could read and there were no printed books. So the churches were like colorful picture books of the stories of the Bible and of the lives of the saints. Everyone could understand them. The child of today learns much from them. As he looks at the image of some saint who has been brave and strong in face

Saint Patrick's Cathedral in New York

of trials, he prays that he too may be unafraid and loyal whatever God calls him to do or dare. He honors the saints and asks them to pray to God for him.

In most Catholic churches there are fourteen pictures, or sculptures, seven on each side. These represent the events of the last day of the life of Jesus, when He went from Pilate's house, where He had been condemned to death, to Calvary, the hill where He was crucified. Above each painting or sculpture there is a wooden cross, called a "Station of the Cross."

Often, especially during Holy Week, a child goes with his parents, and led by the priest, they make that journey as Jesus made it. They go from picture to picture and stop before each station for thought and a brief prayer of repentance and love.

The church is always open, so that one may enter whenever he wishes and "make a visit to Jesus." Within the church, God is found. At the entrance there is a font of water which has been blessed by the priest with solemn prayer. As if to renew the rite of his baptism the Catholic child dips his fingers in the water, makes the sign of the cross and says, "In the name of the Father and of the Son and of the Holy Ghost." By this ceremony he symbolizes that he is once more cleansed of sin and fit to come into God's presence.

He touches his knee to the floor as he faces the altar in adoration of the Blessed Sacrament. He may stop before the image of a saint and pray. At the side altar, he may light a votive candle; as long as it burns, it will carry his prayer to the ear of God and the saints in heaven. He bends the knee and blesses himself again at the altar rail, as always when he passes in front of the altar, and goes out quietly, stopping to use the holy water once more, and, should he feel so inclined, to drop a gift into the poor box.

He loves the stories his mother tells him about the saints. One of the favorites is about St. Christopher who lived soon after the time of Jesus. He grew to be so large and so strong that he could not find any one to serve who was strong and brave as him-

Interior of Catholic Church showing center aisle that leads to altar, symbolic of the path of life that leads to God.

self. Then he heard about Jesus, and decided he would be His servant. He took as his work carrying people across a raging stream where there could not be a ferry and there was no bridge. One day he took a child on his strong back. He seemed a light load at first, but as they went further into the stream, the burden grew heavier and heavier; the man almost feared he could not reach the other shore. He asked the child how it was that he had grown so heavy, and he answered that He was the Christ, and that He was bearing all the sufferings and trials of the world. The man found this hard to believe but the child told him to stick his strong staff in the ground; he did so, and the next morning, he found it had become a palm tree, loaded with dates. Ever since he has been called St. Christopher, the bearer of the Christ. There is a very old saying: "Whosoever shall behold the image of St. Christopher shall not faint or fall on that day."

Best of all is the story of St. George, who slew a fierce dragon. This dragon had its lair in a swamp near a town. Every day the people gave it two sheep to keep it from coming into the town. Finally they had no more sheep. They knew they would have to give it a human victim, and they cast lots. The lot fell upon the King's daughter. The child, dressed like a bride, was taken out to the marsh and left to wait for the dragon. Just then, a knight chanced to ride by. He asked the princess why she was there. She told him, and urged him to hurry away or the dragon would eat him too. He refused to leave her. Soon the dragon appeared. St. George made the sign of the cross, and charged the dragon, piercing him with his lance. There was great rejoicing in the town and the king offered the knight half his kingdom, but he rode on, saying that he must be about his work. St. George is the patron of all who are gallant and brave and kind.

70

MASS: THE HOLY COMMUNION

In the school and in his home, the child is prepared to share in the supreme act of Catholic worship, the sacrifice of the Mass. Every Catholic is obliged to attend Mass every Sunday, and on Holy Days of Obligation.

The Mass is re-enacting the Last Supper which Jesus ate with His disciples, when He gave them His body and blood as bread and wine, and then said, "Do this in commemoration of Me." But the Mass is even more. In it, Christ again offers Himself to God as a sacrifice for sin. The substance of the bread and wine is changed into the substance of the body and blood of Christ, so that he who receives the Holy Sacrament, actually receives the Saviour, Himself.

The meaning of the altar is explained to every Catholic child. An altar is a place where sacrifices are offered to God. In many primitive religions, animals have been burned upon the altar, in the belief that such a sacrifice makes right any wrong one may have done. But Christians believe that when Jesus died upon the cross, His death was an offering sufficient for all the sins of men. Whenever men sin, He is crucified afresh and He sacrifices Himself repeatedly in the Mass that those who repent may find salvation through Him. So, in a Catholic Church as in other places of worship, the altar is central; it is, in a sense, Calvary itself.

The top of the altar is a long narrow stone, covered by three cloths. On either side of the center are candles, large and small, and often a seven-branched candlestick. The number of candles lighted depends upon the solemnity of the Mass. At the right, is the Missal, a book containing the ritual of the Mass. In the central place at the rear stands the tabernacle, a strong locked box, in which is the ciborium, a gold or gold-lined vessel shaped like a goblet with a cover. This contains the bread of the sacrament. The ever-burning sanctuary lamp symbolizes the real presence of the Lord's Body under the appearance of the bread. Above the tabernacle is a crucifix.

The Elevation of the Host. This is the most important part of the Mass.

The Mass

The priest takes the Sacred Host and recites: "Lord, I am not worthy." The people recite the aspiration: "My Lord and My God." Then the priest distributes Holy Communion.

If he lives in a large town, a Catholic child often goes to a parochial school. Religion is a vital part of the training. Each session opens and closes with prayer. There are classes in Bible and Church history and in the catechism. The catechism is a book of questions with answers which state briefly and clearly the teaching of the Church and explain its sacraments. Hymns are learned in the singing classes. All this is in addition to the subjects which are taught in all elementary and high schools.

Registration day in a parochial school.

Most of the teachers are Sisters, members of some religious order. When they were young girls, they dedicated themselves to the work of the Church; they gave up all thought of marrying and having families of their own in order that they might serve Christ with all their powers. They live in a convent and receive very little salary for their work as teachers.

NUNS AND MONKS

There are many different orders of nuns and monks. Each order has its own characteristic rule and wears a particular habit which distinguishes it. For the women these were usually the clothes commonly worn at the time and in the country where the order was founded.

The name "monk" comes from the Greek word meaning "alone," and all monks and nuns, to a certain extent, live in retirement from the world. Their ideal is to love God in the highest degree possible, and to help them achieve this, they take three solemn vows of poverty, chastity and obedience.

The most famous monk of all time was St. Benedict. He lived in the sixth century and he drew up a pattern that has been used as a model for life in monasteries ever since. It is called the Rule of St. Benedict. One of the most appealing pages applied to hospitality. All guests who came to his monasteries had to be treated as though they were Christ for He Himself said: "I was a stranger and ye took me in." In Benedict's day, inns were scarce and travelers had to depend on the monasteries for food and shelter, so that often this rule put the monks to a severe test. Another page applied to manual labor in which "at fixed times the brothers ought to be occupied." St. Benedict had great understanding for human weakness and his success was largely due to his wisdom in adapting his ideas to the ability of the average monk. "Let all things be done with moderation, however, on account of the faint-hearted." Benedict also founded monasteries for women. His sister, Scholastica, was the first abbess.

In medieval times the monastery was the only center of Christian life and teaching. The monks preserved the classics as well as religious writings by copying them painstakingly by hand. They spent many extra hours embellishing some of them with little gilded figures and colored decorations. Among them was the beautiful Book of Kells, now in Trinity College, Dublin.

The nuns have always been noted for their needlework and to-

day, as in the day of Benedict, they embroider vestments and altar linen, and since it is for the service of God, they take every stitch with exquisite care.

In early days monks and nuns lived mostly within their monastery and convent walls, but gradually their rule changed to suit the needs of the times. Today, while there are still a few purely contemplative orders, most communities devote themselves to teaching, nursing and missionary work in every country of the world. All orders spend much time in prayer and have an annual retreat of eight days. The rule of silence is general. A monk or nun rarely speaks unnecessarily.

These active orders are generally admired for their good works. In our own country, the familiar figure of the Franciscan distributing food to the hungry, the Little Sister of the Poor going about her daily work, and the Sister of Charity visiting the sick create a feeling of good will among people of all faiths or none. But in a world where success is measured by material gain, many people feel that the cloistered monks such as the Trappists and nuns like the Carmelites, who devote their lives to meditation and prayer, serve no purpose.

However some of the greatest poets in the world did not think this. Wordsworth knew the spiritual power that solitude fosters when he wrote "The world is too much with us." And the Catholic, in sorrow and despair, is comforted to know he may ask these cloistered orders to pray for him and that "more things are wrought by prayer than this world dreams of."

The age at which a girl may become a nun varies according to the community, but in most convents girls must be eighteen years old before they can take their "simple vows." Then they live the life of a sister and see it in all its phases, though they are not allowed to take solemn vows for three years. The solemn vows bind them irrevocably to the religious life, but during the three years preceding, the novice may leave the convent at any time if she decides that she is not fitted for the vocation. There are only a few convents in the United States today where nuns take solemn vows.

THE FIRST COMMUNION

When the child "attains the age of reason" at seven or eight, he is given special instruction to prepare him for his first Holy Communion. He is taught that a sacrament is "an outward sign of an inward grace," a sign to show to the eyes and ears what is going on inside the soul that receives it.

More than the child can be taught by words, he has learned by watching the celebration of the Mass, almost since babyhood.

He sees the priest approaching the altar, preceded by an altar boy in black cassock, usually with white surplice. The priest's rich vestments show that he is set off from other men. Before the altar he chants prayers of praise and confession and intones readings from the Bible. A choir may join in some of the chants, but there is no solo to draw attention from the altar to the singer and to interrupt the mood of worship.

The priest raises a chalice of wine and a little plate upon which rests the thin round wafer of bread, and prays. The prayer closes with the words of Jesus. "Take ye and eat ye all of this, for this is My Body." Bending the knee, bowing down, the priest receives the wafer and then drinks from the chalice.

For the child in the congregation, following intently all of the service, looking above the priest to the crucifix, the voice is no longer that of the priest but of the figure on the cross, saying, "This is My Body," and a moment later, "This is the chalice of My Blood." And he silently responds, as he has been taught: "My Lord and My God."

The children, who are to receive their first Holy Communion, come forward with hands held together in prayer, kneel at the altar rail and say the Confession. The priest places the Consecrated Host, which to the Catholic is Jesus Christ Himself, upon the tongue of each, saying: "May this Body of our Lord Jesus Christ keep thy soul unto life everlasting. Amen."

To be worthy to receive Holy Communion, a child has had nothing to eat or drink since midnight; one would not have earthly

Receive, O Holy Father

food mixed with the Divine. He has also received the Sacrament of Penance, that he may come free from sin. For this he has gone to the church to pray alone, to think of God's commandments and of his own behavior, and to look at the record which his conscience had made. Where he has done wrong or left undone some good deed he might have done, he is sincerely sorry and makes up his mind that he will not sin in that way again. Then he is ready to go to confession.

CONFESSION

The confessional occupies a prominent place in every Catholic church. It is a closet or box, divided into two parts with a screened opening in the partition. Open confessionals are sometimes used for special occasions. The priest sits on one side and the penitent kneels on the other. Making the sign of the cross, he says, "Bless me, Father, for I have sinned," and tells the priest all that he has on his conscience. Every Catholic is obliged to go to confession one a year, but most people go oftener.

The priest helps him to see where he has made his mistakes and to know how to meet any such temptations should they come again. He encourages and strengthens him. Then he gives some penance, usually to say certain prayers a number of times. The penitent says: "O my God, I am heartily sorry for having offended Thee, and I detest all my sins because I dread the loss of heaven and the pains of hell; but most of all because they offend Thee, my God, who art all-good and deserving of all my love. I firmly resolve, with the help of Thy grace, to sin no more and to avoid near occasions of sin."

The priest raises his hand with the words: "May our Lord Jesus Christ absolve thee; and I absolve thee from thy sins in the name of the Father and of the Son and of the Holy Ghost. Amen." The worshipper, pure in God's sight, leaves the confessional, but stops in the church to thank God for His healing grace and to do his penance.

"Bless me, Father, for I have sinned."

First Communion

Rehearsing for Confirmation. The priest is explaining the seven gifts of the Holy Ghost—wisdom, understanding, counsel, fortitude, knowledge, piety, fear of the Lord.

CONFIRMATION AND OTHER SACRAMENTS

Confirmation is the next sacrament which the Catholic child receives. This ceremony, which is always very beautiful, usually occurs when he is about twelve years old, able to understand its meaning, and to receive it of his own free will. Only a Bishop can administer this sacrament. As the Bishop lays his hand upon the head of the candidate he passes on to him the Holy Ghost who gives to the one who receives Him grace to become a "strong and perfect Christian" and a "soldier of Christ."

This repeats the experience of the earliest followers of Jesus. They had been frightened by His death and were uncertain what to do even after His resurrection. But when He had returned to His Father in Heaven He sent down upon them the Holy Ghost. They were no longer afraid; they were ready to tell all the world about Christ, ready to suffer and die for Him.

The Bishop wears his richest vestments for the ceremony. The candidates for confirmation kneel before him at the altar rail. After offering the prayers ordained for this rite, the Bishop makes the sign of the cross on the forehead of each one with holy oil, saying: "I sign thee with the sign of the cross and I confirm thee with the chrism of salvation, in the name of the Father and of the Son and of the Holy Ghost." He then strikes the child's cheek lightly to remind him that as a soldier of Jesus Christ he may have to suffer.

Both for Confirmation and First Communion, the boys wear ordinary suits of blue or white, as may be decided for the group. The girls wear white dresses and white veils or wreaths of flowers in their hair, for no woman ever enters a Catholic church with her head uncovered. After the service there is usually a celebration at home with gifts and good wishes.

Besides Baptism, Confession, Holy Communion, and Confirmation, there are three other sacraments, making seven in all. These are Matrimony, Ordination, for those who are to become ministers of the Church, and Extreme Unction, the last anointing of one in danger of death.

The cope, worn by the Bishop in processions and at all sacred functions.

The mitre, the official head-dress of the Bishop. It is usually made of white linen, silk or satin, often embroidered or jewelled. The streamers hang down the back.

For both the first Communion and Confirmation the girls wear white.

FESTIVALS OF THE CHURCH

The Catholic Church has many festivals, celebrating events in the life of our Lord and the Blessed Mother and honoring the apostles and the most illustrious saints. Certain parts of the Mass are changed to suit the occasion and direct the thought of the congregation to the person or event or truth which the day commemorates.

The most beloved and universal festival is Christmas. The name, Christ's Mass, comes from the feast of the Catholic Church in honor of the birth of the Christ Child. All the riches of the church are used to give expression to the joy in the Savior's birth. Greens and flowers decorate the building; lights glow upon the altar; the richest vestments are worn; the most fragrant incense burned; joyous hymns are sung. There is a representation of the stable of Bethlehem, with figures of the Child in the manger, His Blessed Mother, St. Joseph, the shepherds with their sheep, the Wise Men bearing gifts, the ox and the ass, and the angels above.

EASTER

Not all the festivals of the Church are days of rejoicing; there are also times of sorrow and penance and fasting. The longest of these is Lent, named from an old word for spring. It comes before Easter and calls to remembrance the forty days which Jesus spent in prayer and fasting in the wilderness before He began His public work.

The first day of Lent is Ash Wednesday. Children come to church before they go to school. The people approach the altar rail, where the priest, dipping his thumb into ashes, marks upon the forehead of each the sign of the cross, and says "Remember, man, that thou art dust and unto dust shalt thou return." This signifies repentance, for in olden times, when men repented, they put sack-cloth on their bodies and sprinkled themselves with ashes. The ashes used on Ash Wednesday came from burning some of the palms which were blessed on Palm Sunday the year before. Then the ashes were

The most beloved and universal festival is Christmas.

blessed with ancient prayers, sprinkled with holy water, perfumed with incense, and put into containers to be kept until needed.

During Lent, Catholics express their penitence in self-denial and fasting. The Lenten Masses omit songs of joy and praise and substitute prayers of repentance. The color of the vestments is violet. During the last two weeks, the images of the churches are covered with purple veils.

The last Sunday of Lent is Palm Sunday. Palms are given out at the services. Often the big leaves have been cut into narrow strips, and one end of each folded over to make a cross. This celebration commemorates the triumphal entry of Jesus into Jerusalem on the first day of His last week, when a great multitude went out befor Him, waving branches and strewing them in His path and crying out, "Blessed is He that cometh in the name of the Lord! Hosanna in the highest!"

Many of the larger churches conduct the impressive service called Tenebrae — darkness. Upon the altar is a large candlestick in the form of a cross, with a triangle rising above the arms. Upon this are arranged fifteen candles. The priests or choir chant fourteen penitential psalms. As each is finished, one by one the candles are extinguished, leaving only the uppermost. All other lights are put out during the chanting of the Benedictus. Then the one candle is removed and buried behind the altar. Out of the total darkness there comes the mournful chant: "Christ was made obedient for us, even unto death." Absolute silence follows, broken in a few moments by a low prayer, "Lord, have mercy." Then comes a crash to typify the opening of the tomb, the candle is replaced on the candlestick. "Christ, the Lord, is risen."

On Friday the day of Jesus' death, the priests wear black vestments. During the service the crucifix is taken from the altar and uncovered; the priests kneel three times before it, kiss it in reverence, and place it on the altar steps. Then in silent, solemn procession the worshippers pass and kneel to kiss the crucifix, remembering the supreme sacrifice Christ made on the first Good Friday. In commemoration of this Catholics eat no meat on Fridays.

During the last two weeks of Lent the images in the churches are covered with purple veils.

On Holy Thursday the Host is taken from the altar and placed in the repository.

Easter is celebrated by Masses of triumph and rejoicing.

Saturday is full of expectation. The paschal candle and the baptismal water which is to be used during the year are consecrated. New fire is kindled and blessed, and brought into the church to relight the sanctuary lamp and the candles at the altar. All is ready for Easter, the resurrection morning, which is celebrated by Masses of triumph and rejoicing: "He hath risen from the dead, to die no more."

THE WORLD WIDE CHURCH

All Catholic Churches use Latin, the language of ancient Rome. This reminds everyone that the Church is old and sacred. It also helps one realize that the Church circles the earth and needs a universal language. There is never an hour when the Mass is not being offered on some altar, using the same words in Latin or in the language of the particular country. More Christians belong to the Roman Catholic Church than to any other. In our country many children are given copies of the prayer-book which contain English translations so that they can assist at the Mass by following with mind and spirit all that the priest does or says in the sacred ceremonies. The scriptures are read in English and the sermon is preached in it.

Everything in the Catholic Church has a spiritual meaning — the flickering of the white candles, the images, the richness and colors of the vestments and the solemn movements of the priest, the very lines, light, and shadows of the building itself. Catholics love to hear the rich intoning of the service. They bow in adoration, humility, quietness of soul. Here each one may find the living God as his God whom he may trust. He knows himself one of a great company of believers. He has hope of eternal life through Christ. All this the Roman Catholic Church makes possible for her people.

THE PROTESTANT WAY

There are other Christians who are called Protestants. They were given that name because they protested against the idea that the Pope in Rome has authority over all Christians, and that the Catholic way of worshipping God is the only right way. Jesus thought there was a simple way to please and serve God without following all the detailed laws of the Jews in His time, and Protestants think that God can be worshipped much more simply than in the Catholic Mass.

The Pilgrim Fathers were Protestants. Their little white meeting houses, with broad steps, high columns, and spires rising among the trees of an open square, were the first churches of New England. Every Sunday, and at least once during the week, the people gathered to talk about God and to worship Him. They met one another; they met God; so the church was their meeting house.

The Pilgrims had come to a new land in which they might be free to worship God according to their own consciences. They wanted to start here a new way of life, ruled not by kings nor by priests, but by the people themselves who would follow the laws of God. When an important decision was to be made, they gathered in the meeting house to discuss the matter; everyone had the right to speak. So the American idea of democracy began in religion.

Although the Pilgrims cared so much for freedom, their religion was strict and exacting. Their churches were without any pictures on the walls, or stained glass in the windows. There was no beautiful ritual to make it easier to sit still through the two long sermons every Sunday. They obeyed rigidly the old commandment for the Sabbath, "Thou shalt not do any work," but there was no festive mood like that of the Jewish Sabbath. Little children found Sunday a hard day. After a while, as the settlers made themselves at home in the new land, life became easier and more gracious, and gradually their observance of the Sabbath became less strict.

VARIETY IN PROTESTANT CHURCHES

Today there are Protestant churches all over the country built like the old meeting houses of New England, but there are many other styles of buildings, too. This variety in buildings is one of the differences between Protestant places of worship and Jewish and Catholic. However different the outside may be, most Jewish synagogues are alike in the general arrangement inside the building, the forms of service, and the language used. So are the Catholic churches. Protestant churches are not alike except that there is always a large room with pews, and at one end, a platform with a pulpit and a Bible on it.

Some Protestant churches are cross-shaped like Catholic churches; often there are side aisles, with seats down the center; sometimes the seats are arranged in a half-circle. In large churches there are galleries. The interior is planned to be practical, so that the congregation can see and hear easily. The preacher, like Jesus in Galilee, gathers his people as closely around him as possible.

Except in a few denominations, each minister plans his own program for the Sunday service of worship: even in the same church it may be slightly different from week to week. The minister does not always wear a robe; if he does, it is black and has no trimmings. He wears it so as not to attract attention to his clothing rather than for any symbolic meaning. English is used for all of the service, except when the members of the church have come from foreign countries. Then they may use the language of their home country. There are Protestant churches in America where German, Swedish, Czech and many other languages are heard. Each church tries to meet the needs of its own community.

For Protestants, the Bible takes the place of the Church as the final authority. They study it and listen to what God says to them through it. It is the business of ministers and teachers to help people understand the parts that puzzle them, but each one must be left free to interpret as he believes right. Some things in the Bible are hard to understand, but the Protestant Church has always believed that what is most important is so clear that even people without much education can find it.

The result is that there are many differences of opinion among Protestants, and many divisions, called denominations. Among them are Lutherans, named for the pioneer reformer Martin Luther who established the church; Presbyterians, who have "Presbyters" (elders) in charge of their administration; Congregationalists who believe that each congregation should govern itself; Baptists who practice immersion and believe that only adults should be baptized; Methodists, who were called by that name because of their strict observance of religious duties. The Episcopal Church is Protestant in that it does not accept the authority of the Pope, and is Catholic in that it does hold some of the ancient traditions, uses a prayer-book, and has an elaborate ritual. At the other extreme are the Friends.

The Protestant church may be very plain or it may be richly decorated, but there are no images to be venerated. There may be a cross on the altar, but there is never the figure of Jesus upon it. There are no confessionals. The congregation shares in the readings and prayers and songs. When there is communion, every member partakes of it; there are no Masses in which the priest alone receives the consecrated bread and wine. From these things we recognize a Protestant Church.

BAPTISM

Not many Protestant children can remember when they first went to Church. In most denominations their parents take them to be baptized by the minister before they are a year old.

Interior of old New England church

The baptism is part of the regular church service on the special Sunday that is set aside for it. After the opening hymns and prayers, the choir and congregation begin to sing softly:

"I think when I read that sweet story of old
When Jesus was here among men,
How He called little children as lambs to His fold
I should like to have been with Him then."

The minister waits beside the baptismal font and one of the officers of the church leads the parents in. The father carries the baby, and both parents stand before the minister who asks them to promise to teach their child to love God and to train him to live in the way that Jesus taught.

Sometimes the minister takes the baby in his arms, as Jesus took little children to bless them. Then he dips his fingers into the water and lays his hand on the child's head, and calls him by name as he speaks the same baptismal words the Catholics use: "I baptize thee in the name of the Father and of the Son and of the Holy Ghost."

Often several babies are baptized at the same service.

Some Protestant churches do not think it is right to baptize a child until he is old enough to know what it means. Baptism is a symbol of purity, of washing away of sin. What can a little child know of this? So they wait until the child is twelve or older and understands what it means to accept the Christian faith. Most churches that have this idea also think the right way to baptize is to immerse the person entirely under water. So they have baptistries, small pools, built into their churches, or they go to some stream for the ceremony. For them immersion symbolizes that the sinful or selfish person has died to sin, is buried under the water and is raised up a new person, dedicated to the new way of life which Jesus taught.

Episcopal baptism service.

THE PROTESTANT HOME

Protestant churches, like all others, teach that a parent's first responsibility is the training of his children. In families where God is loved, the little child is put to bed with a prayer. When he is a little older, he learns to repeat a prayer himself. One favorite with Protestant children is:

"Jesus, tender Shepherd, hear me;
Bless thy little lamb tonight;
Through the darkness be Thou near me;
Keep me safe till morning light.

"All this day Thy hand has led me,
And I thank Thee for Thy care;
Thou hast clothed me, warmed and fed me;
Listen to my evening prayer!"

Usually he follows the memorized prayer with an informal one, for he is taught to use his own thoughts and words as he prays.

The child learns to think of God as the Giver of all good things, and it helps to make him feel secure in God's world.

In some families the Bible is read aloud every day, or at least on Sundays, each one taking a verse in turn. In this way the stories and the wisdom of this wonderful Book come to be well known, and its perfect language helps the children learn to speak well. Sometimes they memorize favorite verses from the Psalms, such as: "I will lift up mine eyes unto the hills, from whence cometh my help," or "My help cometh from the Lord, which made heaven and earth," or "As the mountains are round about Jerusalem, so the Lord is round about His people, from henceforth even forever." These are words in which the Hebrew poets express their confidence in God's care. As they grow older, the children are encouraged to read and study the Bible for themselves, and to pray and talk to God about their problems. They may pray whenever they wish and say whatever they want to say.

"The Lord is my shepherd; I shall not want."

"*. . . and help me to be a good boy, Amen.*"

In families where God is loved, the little child is put to bed with a prayer.

There is a grace said at meals in many Protestant homes, sometimes by the father in whatever words he may choose; sometimes it is one that the children have learned and repeat together, such as:

"For food and rest and loving care
And all that makes the world so fair
We thank thee, Lord."

Protestants, like Jews, believe that religion is a way of life; it is thinking of God in whatever one does. Luther, the father of Protestants, taught, "A cobbler, a smith, a peasant has his own calling as much as the priest. Every one must serve the rest so that all may work together for the common good." The Protestant has no forms to use, but his ideal is to show his love for God in whatever he does. No matter how far he may fall short of the ideal, he truly tries to follow the teachings of Jesus, who said, "Be ye perfect, as your Father is perfect."

THE CHURCH SCHOOL

When he is four or five years old, the Protestant child begins to go to the Church School, which is held on Sunday mornings before, during or after the worship of the church.

The school is divided into departments, according to age. In each department there is an opening service of worship, followed by talking and study and handwork. The child is taught that God is near him, not just on Sunday and in the church, but every day, wherever he goes. He is taught to think of God's plan to make the world beautiful and friendly and to think of ways in which he can help. He hears stories of Jesus, the friend of little children, and of the heroes of the Jewish and Christian faiths. When he is old enough he studies the Bible and memorizes parts of it.

On one side of the room, a small table stands as an altar, a center for worship. Upon it are a cross, the Bible, flowers and candles. Two children are chosen to light the candles each Sunday.

110

In many Protestant homes a grace is said at meals.

As they do so in the Primary Department, all the group may repeat, "God said, 'Let there be light,' and there was light." And when the candles are burning brightly, as the ones who have lighted them return to their seats, all recite:

"Thou wilt light my candle."
"Send out Thy light and Thy truth; let them lead me."

Then there is a service of thanksgiving, in which the children work out a litany of their own or use one they planned an earlier Sunday, such as:

"We are glad we have fathers and mothers to take care of us:
We are glad we have warm clothes to wear.
God is very good to us.

"We are glad we have friends to play with:
We are glad we have teachers to teach us.
God is very good to us.

"We are glad we can see the blue sky which makes our world beautiful.
We are glad we have day and night for play and rest.
Thank you, God, for all these things.
God is very good to us."

Perhaps, as they have been talking about God's care for His children, the teacher has said for them the twenty-third Psalm:

"The Lord is my shepherd; I shall not want.
He maketh me to lie down in green pastures;
He leadeth me beside the still waters."

Then they may go to low tables for handwork and draw pictures of sheep or fold tents for the shepherds. As they work, they talk freely and the teacher is there to ask or answer questions.

One of the favorite hymns of this group is:

112

"But Jesus said, Suffer little children to come unto me . . . for of such is the king-dom of heaven."

In each department there is an opening service of worship . . . the child is taught that God is near him, not just on Sunday and in the Church, but every day, wherever he goes.

Beginners bow their heads for closing prayer. Sometimes they repeat the Mizpah benediction: "May the Lord watch between me and thee while we are absent one from the other."

The minister is the friend of every child in the Sunday school.

"How strong and sweet my Father's care
That round about me like the air,
Is with me always, everywhere.
He cares for me."

The older boys and girls learn about the people who wrote the Bible, their customs and ways of thinking, and the country in which they lived. They study maps of Palestine. They find pictures and articles which show the fascinating discoveries which have been made as scholars have dug among the ruins of ancient cities, and learn from them about the way people lived in olden times. This group uses a work-book which directs their study as they read the Bible itself.

When they are learning what Moses did for his people, they memorize the Ten Commandments which he gave them. When they read about David, the shepherd boy, who became the greatest king of Israel, they learn the twenty-third psalm and some of the other psalms which it is believed he wrote. They think of Jesus as He lived in Palestine, walking along roads they can trace on their maps, and teaching beside the lake and on the hillsides which they can locate. His parables are vivid sketches of life in His time. They learn the stories in which He spoke of Himself as a good shepherd, risking his own life to find a lost sheep; as a light which helps people see their way safely; as a sower who scatters his seed everywhere, hoping that some of it will take root and grow. Jesus becomes their teacher and leader, their older brother, their friend, whom they love and try to follow.

They memorize the Lord's Prayer, the Beatitudes, the verses in which He told what kind of people are happiest, the Golden Rule, "Whatsoever ye would that men should do unto you, do ye also unto them," and His answer to the question, "What is the first commandment?"

They journey with Paul as he traveled into Turkey, Greece and on to Rome, telling people everywhere the story of Jesus and about the new way of living in love and trust, free from all fear.

The older boys and girls use a work book which directs their study as they read the Bible itself.

They study maps of Palestine.

They learn the words that Paul wrote to the Christians in Corinth which say that love is the greatest thing in the world.

In the Church School the children find out how their own denomination came to be and what it is doing. They hear stories about missionaries, some perhaps young people who have gone from their own Church. In the heart of Asia missionaries are teaching new methods of agriculture and starting small industries which can be carried on at home; on the islands of the Pacific they are publishing books that can be read easily. Wherever they go they tell the good news which Jesus brought to the world. The Protestant child is taught more about these heroes of today than about the saints of the past. He is proud to know that his church believes it must help all people to gain justice and liberty, to live with hope and courage because one God is the Father of all.

THE BIBLE

Although Protestants read and study the Bible more than Catholics do, Catholics and Jews share reverence for the Bible. All of them call it the Word of God. This does not necessarily mean that they believe that God Himself wrote the words or that He told the men who wrote them just what to put down. It does mean that when a person reads the Bible earnestly, he hears God speaking to his heart and his conscience.

The sacred writings of the Jews are that part of the Bible which Christians call the Old Testament; these were the scriptures used by Jesus and His first followers. Soon the Christians began to write; they wanted to keep a record of Jesus' sayings and tell of His life. One wrote an account of the work of the earliest missionaries. Letters were written by some of the leaders. All these were treasured and finally collected into what is called the New Testament.

The Jewish writings were in Hebrew; the earliest Christian ones in Greek; this was the common language of the people at the

Protestants believe that what is most important in the Bible is so clear that anyone can find it.

time. Later the whole Bible was translated into Latin, which is still used in the Catholic Church. The priests copied it over and over again on vellum with great devotion, using colors and tiny illustrations to decorate the pages they loved so well. Some of the very old copies may be seen in museums and libraries today.

The people who could not read Latin could know no more about the Bible than the priests taught them. One English priest, John Wycliffe, translated long stories as part of his sermons. He wanted to put the whole Bible into language all the people could understand. No one had yet learned how to make printed books, and so his translations had to be copied by hand. The few copies were passed around and many people memorized long sections. One woman recited them so well that she was often invited to entertain parties by her recitations.

About a hundred years later, Johann Gutenberg discovered how to print with movable type, and the first book he printed was the Latin Bible. After another hundred years, William Tyndale took up Wycliffe's work of translation and then printed the first New Testament in English. Later the Catholic Church had an English translation of the Bible made which its members now use freely, but when Tyndale was living, the Church taught that the Bible was too sacred for ordinary people to handle and so hard to understand that only the Church could explain it correctly. When a priest criticized Tyndale for making the Bible so common, he replied: "If God spares my life, I will make it possible for a boy that holds a plough to know more of the Scripture than you do."

Since then there have been many translations of the Bible into English. The best loved was done in the reign of King James I of England and is called the King James version. This follows very closely the words which Tyndale had used, so that he is called the "Father of the English Bible."

Wherever Christians have gone, they have carried the Bible with them and it has been translated into the everyday language of the country. In some places where there was no written language, missionaries learned to speak as the natives do. Then they put down letters to represent the sounds and so built up a language in which they could write and which they could teach the people to read. The Bible was the first book written. The study of it has been the beginning of education and civilization for many. Now the Bible is the "Book of a Thousand Tongues." It is the world's best-seller; about thirty million copies are printed every year.

THE SERVICE OF WORSHIP

In some churches there is a special service of worship for children on Sunday in addition to the Church School. In this the children themselves read the Bible, take up the collection, sing in the choir and assist in other ways. In most churches children attend the regular services with their parents. They may not understand all of the sermon, but they can understand and catch the spirit of worship which is even more important. They can join with the congregation in singing the Doxology:

> "Praise God from whom all blessings flow;
> Praise Him all creatures here below;
> Praise Him above, ye heavenly host,
> Praise Father, Son and Holy Ghost."

and the hymn of praise that every Protestant learns to love:

> "Holy, holy, holy! Lord God Almighty!
> Early in the morning our song shall rise to Thee.
> Only Thou art holy; there is none beside Thee
> Perfect in power, in love and purity."

Later in the service come other hymns and an anthem by the choir, or a solo. Protestants sing more than the people of any other religious group, and the children have a share in the worship and come to know and love hymns that have come from many countries and belong to all Christians.

The congregation shares also in the reading from the Bible; the first selection is usually a psalm, read responsively.

There are prayers, in which the minister tries in his own words to make the people conscious of God's presence and to express for them their deepest needs and hopes. One of these closes with the Lord's Prayer, in which all join.

The organist plays while the congregation makes its offering. This continues the very old custom of bringing gifts to the altar as part of the worship of God.

The sermon is more important in Protestant churches than in others. This is true because each person has greater freedom and more responsibility. There is no priest to tell him what he should think or do; there are no fixed religious customs to control his behaviour. So he needs more help that he may understand the meaning of the Bible, and of Christ's life and work, and that he may want to share in all that is right and beautiful.

After the sermon, a prayer, and another hymn, the minister pronounces the bendiction. Frequently he will use the age-old Jewish blessing:

> "The Lord bless thee and keep thee;
> The Lord make his face to shine upon thee
> And be gracious unto thee;
> The Lord lift up his countenance upon thee
> And give thee peace."

or the beautiful words of Paul:

> "The grace of the Lord Jesus Christ,
> the love of God, and the communion
> of the Holy Spirit be with you all."

A moment of silent prayer, and the service is over. Friendly chatting begins as the people leave their seats. The minister stands at the door to greet them instead of withdrawing into some inner room. There is a general air of informality that is typically Protestant.

124

The family pew

JOINING THE CHURCH

When Jesus was twelve years old, He went to the Temple in Jerusalem, for according to the custom of the Jews, He had become Bar Mitzvah, a son of the commandment. Following this example the Protestant Church as well as the Catholic, plans for the confirmation of its boys and girls at about this age. Protestant churches do not consider this a sacrament in the way the Catholics do. They recognize that God's love has been around these children all their lives, His Spirit always near to help them, but now they are old enough to take more responsibility for their own behaviour and for the Church, as both Jews and Catholics have taught, and to give themselves by their own free choice in love and loyalty to their Heavenly Father.

In many churches the minister has a special class to teach these older boys and girls what it means to be a Christian and a member of this church. Then at a regular Sunday service, they come to the front of the room and those who have not been baptized as babies receive that sacrament now. Following this they all promise to help the church by their attendance, their work, their money, and most of all their way of living. The minister gives each one the right hand of fellowship, and then the congregation rises to welcome the new group.

The new members then receive the communion for the first time. This is most often spoken of as the Lord's Supper. It is more simple than the Catholic Mass. All church members are invited to share in it. The table in front of the pulpit has been set with plates of bread and cups of wine. The minister reads the story of Jesus' last supper, as the Catholic priest does at Mass, offers a prayer, and breaks the bread. Then the deacons or elders pass first the bread and later, the wine, to the people in the pews, who bow in prayer as they receive them.

Protestants do not think that there is any miraculous change in the bread and wine during the ceremony so that they become the

At all the regular services the organist plays the great music of the church, and sometimes gives special recitals.

actual body and blood of Christ. They believe that the service is a symbol of His spiritual presence.

The Lord's Supper is also a communion of Christians with one another. We always feel that we are friends of those who sit down with us at a dinner table. Nothing makes us more at home than to eat a meal together. So the "Supper" to which Jesus invites all his friends, makes them conscious of their fellowship with one another.

For many Protestant children, the church is a second home. Here they learn to be a part of a larger family of friends, each of whom wants all the others to find life good and has a share in making it so. Besides the services of worship and study on Sunday, there are group meetings of boys and girls of different ages to discuss questions which interest them and to carry on projects of service for their communities or the missionary work of their church. There are suppers and parties; there are clubs of many sorts. There are summer conferences and camps, where the boys and girls work and play, study and worship together. They try to understand what it means to be a Christian, to accept for their own lives the way of struggle and suffering in the service of others, the way of forgiveness and reconciliation, the way of the cross.

FESTIVALS OF THE CHURCH

There are fewer festivals in the Protestant churches than either the Jews or the Catholics have, but there are some special days for which to plan. Most important of all are Christmas and New Year and Easter.

For Christmas there is often a creche, in Protestant as in Catholic churches. Always there are greens, candles, and a star. There are special services when the carols which celebrate the Saviour's birth are sung by the children, the congregation, and the choir. These come from many countries; some are very old. "O come, all ye faithful," is a Latin hymn, written three hundred years ago

and translated into very many languages. "Silent night, holy night" was written in a mountain village of Austria a hundred years ago and has been loved wherever Christians celebrate the birth of their Lord.

Early Christmas morning or the evening before, groups of young people often go out caroling, stopping especially at the homes of those who are not able to come to the services. At the Sunday School Christmas party Santa Claus comes, sometimes to bring a present for each child, sometimes to take the gifts which the children have brought to send to others.

On New Year's Eve, many churches have a watch night service. It is a solemn service, though not so serious as that of the Jewish New Year. The people gather to think of the year that is gone, to ask for forgiveness for what has been wrong and for strength and wisdom to do better in the year ahead, and to remember once more that, whatever may happen, God's love will be ever about them.

Many Protestants join with Catholics in the observance of Lent. They give up something which they usually do in order to have more money to give to Christ's work, or more time to think about Him, or just to have a little practice in self-denial. When the Thursday evening of Holy Week comes, they gather for a special communion service, to remember Jesus' last supper with His disciples. They think of Jesus' infinite tender pity for all who sin and suffer and the brave quietness of spirit which made Him ready to give His life to do His Father's will. How Christ saves men, they may not be able to explain, but they have found it true that their weakness and desire to do things that are wrong disappear when they think of His boundless love, stronger than sin and death.

Easter is the day of joy. An early service to welcome the sunrise is often held, for it was early in the morning on the first day of the week that Jesus' friends found His tomb empty. At the regular service there are flowers, always the symbol of life, white lilies with their purity and fragrance. Their sweetness fills the room, even as the influence of His life has reached far beyond the little land of Palestine, where He lived and died. Because of Him, men

130

"O come, all ye faithful . . ."

find it easier to believe that love is stronger than hate, life is more enduring than death.

In the faith and hope that came to the world on a Sunday so long ago the Christian church had its birth. From that small beginning it has grown and it believes it will continue to grow until all men are drawn into the one family of which Christ is the elder brother. The Protestant churches look always for new ways to make life come closer to that dream.

THE FRIENDS

The Society of Friends is the group which emphasizes most the presence of the Spirit which they call the "Inner Light." Every person has a conscience which tells him what is right; if he listens for this inner voice and follows what it says, he will find it speaks ever more clearly. He can learn much from others but he is responsible for his own behavior; he cannot give that responsibility to any priest or teacher. Jesus said, "Not every one that saith unto me, 'Lord, Lord,' shall enter into the kingdom of heaven but he that doeth the will of my Father." Therefore the Friends do not ask a member what he believes, nor require him to follow any religious form. They never try to make other people agree with them. They want liberty for themselves and they give liberty to others. They expect Friends to follow the Inner Light and to treat every other person as a child of God.

The Friends go back to the simplicity of the religion which Jesus Himself taught. When they meet for worship on the first day of the week, they gather in a very plain building. There are no decorations and there is no pulpit. There is no program arranged beforehand. There is no minister in charge.

The people come in and take their seats in silence. They believe that when men sit together in quiet and compose their souls, the truth emerges. If someone thinks that God has said something to him which would help the others too, he rises and speaks, even though he is only a child. No one has special authority to speak, except God Himself, but all are willing to listen to what anyone says. Then in silence again, each one considers whether what was said seems true to him; if not, he can forget it.

When it is time to close the meeting, one of the older members rises, shakes hands with the person next to him, calls him "Friend" and others do the same. Each one goes away, certain that he has met with God as well as with his friends.

The Friends believe in giving as little thought as possible to their clothes. In the early days of their history, they adopted very simple costumes. When all dressed alike, no one could make a display or have foolish pride in his appearance, and no poor person was uncomfortable. After a while these costumes were quite out of style, and the Friends, or Quakers, as they were also called, became conspicuous. So most of them today have given up the costume, but they dress and live simply that they may have more to give to relieve the suffering of others. Their Service Committee has fed the hungry and clothed the naked, especially in wartime.

Protestant churches are many and varied. Protestants do not want uniformity. They think that growth and progress come through independence and free initiative. Sometimes one group is sure that its way is the only right way; but that is not the true Protestant spirit. At heart they are one, the society of free individuals who have found God as their Father and are trying to live in the way that Jesus taught. The Protestant churches of China recognized this when they said: "We agree to differ; we resolve to love; we unite to serve." In our country many denominations are united in the Federal Council of Churches of Christ, and associated with other Christians in a World Council of Churches. These organizations can do many things which no one church can do alone.

Protestant churches are many and varied. Protestants do not want uniformity.

●

Religion in America has many forms. Some of us are Catholics, some Jews, some Protestants. Our American life is richer because it has the stately beauty of ancient Judaism, the mother religion of us all; the rich beauty and devout adoration of the Catholic High Mass; the meaningful, solemn silence of a Friends' meeting and the joyous singing of other Protestant congregations.

But although there are differences in our religions, we all agree that there is only one God. We all use the Bible. We all set aside one day in the week for worship. We all honor the Commandments given by Moses. And we all know that they are summed up in two: "Thou shalt love the Lord thy God with all thy heart and soul and mind," and "Thou shalt love thy neighbor as thyself."

●

Candlelight carol service

THE PHOTOGRAPHS

PAGE

Title Page — Arnold Eagle: Boy carrying Torah.

15. Herbert Sonnenfeld: Mother lighting candles.
19. Herbert Sonnenfeld, from Pix: Reading the psalms.
23. Arnold Eagle: Torah.
24. M. L. Markowitz: Boy reading.
25. F. P. G.: Writing Hebrew.
26. Jacob Lofman, from Pix: Reciting prayers.
28. M. L. Markowitz: Bar Mitzvah symbols.
29. Arnold Eagle: Putting on tephillin.
31. Arnold Eagle: Boys around altar.
33. Arnold Eagle: Guard of honor for the Torah.
34. Acme News Pictures: Rabbi.
35. Pix: Learning Hebrew alphabet.
36. Herbert Sonnenfeld: Senior Hebrew class.
37. Heinz H. Weissenstein, courtesy Rabbi Rosenblum, Temple Israel: Reform confirmation.
38. G. A. Douglas, from Gendreau, N. Y.: Temple Emanuel.
41. N. Y. World-Telegram: Boy blowing shofar.
42. Erich Kastan, courtesy Federation of Jewish Philanthropies of N. Y.: Girl gathering corn.
43. Arnold Eagle: Procession of children around altar.
45. Herbert Sonnenfeld: Children watching a Menorah.
46. Herbert Sonnenfeld, courtesy of the Jewish Education Committee: Hebrew anagrams.
47. Herbert Sonnenfeld: Menorah on tower.
49. Albert Steiner, from Black Star: Picking flowers.
50. Acme News Pictures: Kiddush cup.
52. Acme News Pictures: Seder table.
53. Herbert Sonnenfeld, courtesy of the Jewish Education Committee: The four questions.
54. Herbert Sonnenfeld, from Pix: Boy with matzoth.
58. U.P.I. photo: Pope Paul VI (portrait by Bernard Godwin)

PAGE

60. Maryknoll Fathers: Laying on of hands ceremony.
61. Maryknoll Fathers: Prostration.
62. Monkmeyer: St. Peter's.
64. Herbert Sonnenfeld: The Blessed Mother.
67. Ewing Galloway: St. Patrick's.
69. Publicity department, Archdiocese of N. Y.: Church interior.
71. Victor de Palma, from Black Star: Children at wayside shrine.
73. William Rittase, from Liturgical Arts Society: Altar.
74. Ewing Galloway: Elevation of the Host.
75. Maryknoll Fathers: The Mass.
76. Publicity department, Archdiocese of N. Y.: Parochial school.
77. Reverend Justin Costello, St. Catherine of Siena Church: First day of school.
79. Hirz, from Frederick Lewis: Nun in Cloister.
81. Roy Pinney, from Black Star: Missionary.
83. Maryknoll Fathers: Offering the Host.
85. Reverend Justin Costello, St. Catherine of Siena Church: Confession.
86. F.P.G.: First Communion.
86. Publicity department, Archdiocese of N. Y.: Rehearsal for Confirmation.
88. Liturgical Arts Society: Mitre.
88. Liturgical Arts Society: Cope.
89. N. Y. World-Telegram: Girls leaving church.
91. Publicity department, Archdiocese of N. Y.: Nun at crèche.
93. Maryknoll Fathers: Altar images covered for Holy Week.
94. Maryknoll Fathers: Repository.
95. Publicity department, Archdiocese of N. Y.: Easter Service.
97. Paul Parker: Choirboys.
98. F.P.G.: Country church.
101. F. Albert, from Frederic Lewis: New England church.
103. Stewart Love, from F.P.G.: Interior of Old Church.

PAGE

105. National Council of Protestant Episcopal Churches: Baptism.

107. Ellen Johnson: Reading the Bible.

108. Philip Gendreau, N. Y.: Child praying.

109. Paul Parker: Child learning prayer.

111. Jack Delano, F.S.A., Library of Congress: Saying grace.

113. Alfred Eisenstadt, from Pix: Bible stories.

114. Keystone View Company: Sunday School worship service.

114. Ellen Johnson: Children praying.

115. E. Rosskam, Standard Oil Co.: Preacher.

117. Alfred Eisenstadt, from Pix: Boy with Bible.

118. Ellis O. Hinsey, courtesy International Council Religious Education: Boys and girls at work table.

119. Alfred Eisenstadt, from Pix: Sunday School class.

121. Philip Gendreau, N. Y.: Woman reading Bible.

125. National Council of Protestant Episcopal Churches: Family in church.

127. Lilo Kaskel, courtesy Riverside Church: Organist.

129. Paul Parker: Boys singing.

131. Leander S. Miller, courtesy Church of the Ascension: Christmas Eve.

134. Philip Gendreau, N. Y.: Patrick Henry's Church, Richmond.

134. Jack Manning, from Black Star: Little Church Around the the Corner.

135. Marion P. Wolcott, F.S.A., Library of Congress: New Hampshire meeting house.

135. Roy Perry, courtesy National Council of Protestant Episcopal Churches: Westbury Church.

135. Gregor, from Monkmeyer: Hampton Church.

135. Joel Horowitz, from Black Star: Trinity Church, Wall Street.

136. Jacob Lofman, from Pix: Christmas carol service.

INDEX

Abraham 13, 21, 22

Absolution 84

"Age of Reason" 82

Altar 66, 68, 69

Apostles 59

Ark 30

Ash Wednesday 90, 92

Baptism 63, 87, 102, 104, 105, 126

Baptists 102

Bar Mitzvah 27-30, 126

Bedtime prayers 106, 108, 109

Benediction 124

Bible 102, 106, 110, 111, 112, 114, 116, 120, 122, 123, 124, 137

Bishops 59, 87, 88

Blessing 16, 44, 50

Book of Kells 78

Candles 14, 44, 68, 72, 92, 112, 128

Cantor 30, 32

Carols 130, 136

Catechism 76

Choir 30, 35, 97, 104, 123

Christ 59, 65, 70, 72, 78, 87, 92, 96 (See Jesus)

Christening (See Baptism)

Christianity 57, 66

Christmas 44, 90, 91, 128, 130

Church:
  Roman Catholic 66, 90, 96
  Protestant 99

Church buildings 66, 67, 99, 100

Circumcision 20, 21

Communion 82, 126, 130

Confession 40, 82, 84

Confirmation 35, 37, 87, 88, 89

Congregationalists 102

Conservative Jews 35

Convent 78, 79, 80

Covering the head 27, 87

Crèche 128

Cross 68, 128

Crucifix 65, 67, 92

David 20, 30

Day of Atonement 39

Denominations 100, 102

Dietary laws:
  Jewish 18
  Catholic 92

Dispersion of Jews 13, 35, 39, 51

Doxology 123

Easter 22, 90, 96, 130

Elders 102, 128

Episcopalians 105

Esther 44

Eternal Light 30

Everburning Light 72

Extreme Unction 87

Family Observances 14, 16, 18, 20, 40, 44, 48, 55

Fasting 39, 40

Feast of Booths 40

Feast of Weeks 55

Federal Council of Churches 133

Festivals:
  Jewish 39-55
  Catholic 90
  Protestant 128

Festival of First Fruits 55

Festival of Lights 44

Forgiveness 40, 56, 130

Four Questions 53

Freedom of Religion ix, 44, 51, 99

Friends 132, 133

Godparents 20, 63

Golden Rule 18, 120

Good Friday 92

Grace at meals 51, 110, 111
(See Blessing)

Gutenberg, Johann 122

Hail Mary 65

Hallah 14

Hanukah 44

Havdalah 18

Hebrew 22, 25, 32, 36

Hebrews 13

Hillel 18

Holy Ghost (Spirit) 63, 68, 84, 87, 124

Holy Water 68, 102

Holy Week 130

Hospitality 16, 78

Hymns 104, 116, 123, 124, 130

Images 65, 66, 68, 96, 102

Immersion 102, 104

Israel 13, 35, 55

Jerusalem 13, 30, 44, 92

Jesus 56, 57, 68, 70, 72, 82, 87, 99, 104, 106, 110, 112, 116, 120, 126, 130, 132, 133

Jewish History 13, 17, 18, 31, 36, 42, 44, 46, 48, 51

Jewish Laws 17, 18, 20

Jewish Scriptures 22, 32

Joining the Church 126

Judah 13, 30

Judah Maccabee 13, 44

Judgment 39

Kiddush 16

Kingdom of God 57

Kingdom of Heaven 113, 132

Kosher 20

Laying on of hands 59, 60

Lent 90, 92, 130

Lord's Prayer 65, 116, 124

142

Lord's Supper   56, 57, 128, 130
    (See Communion)
Love the Lord, thy God 22, 56, 120
Love thy neighbor   18, 22, 56, 120
Luther, Martin   102, 110
Lutherans   102

Mary, the Blessed Mother 64, 65, 66
Mass   72, 82, 90, 92, 102
Matzoth   48, 55
Meeting house   99
Methodists   102
Minister   100, 104
Missionaries   120
Menorah   44, 45, 47
Monks   78, 80
Moses   13, 17, 20, 22, 35, 51, 116
Mt. Sinai   35

Naming a child 21, 63, 102, 103, 104
New Testament   122
New Year   39, 40, 130
Nuns   78, 80

Old Testament   120
One God   ix, xi, 13, 14, 22,
             35, 120,137
Ordination   61

Palestine 13, 18, 40, 44, 47, 55,
       56, 116, 118, 130
Palm Sunday   90, 92

Passover   22, 48-55, 56
Paul   57, 120
Penance   84
Penitence   39, 84, 92
Pentecost   55, 57
Peter   59
Pilgrim Fathers   99
Pope   58, 59, 102
Prayer 16, 27, 39, 40, 65, 80, 84,
     106, 108, 109, 120, 124
Prayer book   30, 96
Presbyterians   102
Priest   59, 82, 84
Purim   44

Rabbi   16, 27, 32, 35
Reform Jews   35
Rome   59
Rosary   65
Rosh Hashanah   39

Sabbath   14-18, 39, 57
Sacrament 68, 72, 82, 84, 87, 126
Saints   66, 68
St. Benedict   78, 80
St. Christopher   68, 70
St. George   70
St. Joseph   66
Sayings of the Fathers   17
Schools:
  Synagogue   22, 24, 25
  Parochial   76, 77
  Church   110

Seder	22, 48, 52	Tephillin	27, 28, 29
Semites	13	Torah	22, 23, 30-33, 51, 56
Sermon	123, 124	Trafah	20
Shema	22, 27	Tyndale, William	122
Shield of David	30		
Shofar	39, 40		
Sign of the Cross	63, 65, 68, 84, 87, 90	Unleavened bread	48
Succoth	40, 55		
Sunday	46, 57, 72, 99, 100, 123	Vestments	32, 82, 87, 100
Synagogue	16, 17, 19, 25, 30-35, 40, 55		
		Washing hands	16, 20, 51
		World Council of Churches	133
Talith	27, 28	Wycliffe, John	122
Temple	35		
Ten Commandments	17, 35, 55, 116		
Tenebrae	92	Yom Kippur	39, 40